THE DECK BOOK

Inspirational Design Ideas

Melissa Cardona & Hickory Dickory Decks

Schiffer Publishing Ltd

4880 Lower Valley Road, Atglen, PA 19310 USA

Designed by John P. Cheek
Type set in Bell Gothic Black/Bell Gothic BT

ISBN: 978-0-7643-2284-6
Printed in China

Schiffer Books are available at special discounts for bulk purchases for sales promotions or premiums. Special editions, including personalized covers, corporate imprints, and excerpts can be created in large quantities for special needs. For more information contact the publisher:

Published by Schiffer Publishing Ltd.
4880 Lower Valley Road
Atglen, PA 19310
Phone: (610) 593-1777; Fax: (610) 593-2002
E-mail: Info@schifferbooks.com

For the largest selection of fine reference books on this and related subjects, please visit our web site at
www.schifferbooks.com

In Europe, Schiffer books are distributed by
Bushwood Books
6 Marksbury Ave.
Kew Gardens
Surrey TW9 4JF England
Phone: 44 (0) 20 8392 8585; Fax: 44 (0) 20 8392 9876
E-mail: info@bushwoodbooks.co.uk
Website: www.bushwoodbooks.co.uk

Contents

Introduction

Welcome to Hickory Dickory Decks' new deck design book. Together with Schiffer Publishing we have compiled hundreds of decks in this easy-to-reference design guide full of inspiring ideas to help you transform your outdoor living space into a private oasis. Long ago we stopped designing boring rectangle wood decks built to fit an old picnic table and a pair of dirty boots. Today's decks are complete outdoor rooms, with imagination as the only limitation to what can be created. Because life is getting busier for all of us, a quiet retreat or a comfortable place to entertain and relax outdoors is becoming a dream to pursue for many. I hope this book opens your imagination and ideas follow right into your own backyard transformation. Go find your slippers, grab a beverage, relax in your favorite chair, and let us work together to make your dream deck a reality. You may not find the exact deck you're looking for on these pages, instead, borrow ideas from an assortment of your favorites to create your own master-piece.

With over 19 years in the deck business, Hickory Dickory Decks has developed a proven method for helping our customers design their own custom decks. By asking yourself some simple questions, measuring your own home and backyard, working with your existing property's unique personality, and borrowing the odd good idea from other decks, we can work together to create the deck of your dreams while staying in a comfortable budget for your family.

As you browse through this book, ask yourself some questions and start taking some notes. When your information and idea gathering are complete, it's time to either start drawing yourself, or get a professional deck designer/builder to help put your ideas on paper. Then, a proper itemized quote can be done either by the professional builders, or you can take your design to the local deck supplier and price out your materials. The next decision is easy for some, hard for others. Should you call in the pros or invest some of your time in creating a custom deck? As custom deck builders, we hope you choose the pro route, but either way, we hope your custom backyard retreat brings years and years of beautiful memories and helps make your home a more enjoyable place to live.

Of primary concern to the design of your deck is the layout of your home and property. Deciding where to put your dream deck on your property is a good place to start. Is it going to be an access into and out of your home, or will it be built further away in your yard? The closer it is to your home, the more it will be used. Measuring the deck's distance off the ground is another early consideration. Depending on whether your door is two feet or ten feet off the ground, it will lead to two very different looking decks. High decks require railings in order to meet safety standards. At some point you will want to consult with your friendly building inspector, who will help you follow the proper building codes for your area.

Exposure to sun or shade is a major consideration in the design and placement of some decks. If you are a sun worshipper and build a deck in the shade, you probably will not be as happy as having built it in a sunny area. Similarly, someone who prefers a little shade will want to include plans for shade if they can only build their deck with a full southern exposure. Decide which time of day you will be getting most use out of your deck and figure out the sun's location then so you can plan for your ideal sun exposure and layout. You may have to work around some of the things already on your home or in your yard. An air conditioning unit can be moved, but perhaps you can work around it or build toward another area of your yard instead. The same goes for walkways, pools, patios, ponds, driveways, gardens, door exits, and windows, as well as for existing trees, shrubs, grading, and nice views.

The next category to consider in your design planning is your use of the new deck. A cozy spa area may be just what you had in mind for that private party, or for relaxing before bed. Each family member living in the home will have different needs and wants, and it's important to anticipate these needs while designing your deck. You need to ask yourself and your family how your new deck will be used.

Let's start with some easy questions. How many people live in the home, and how many people will you want to entertain on the deck? We suggest a minimum of 25 ft^2 for every person living in your home. The next question to help with sizing your deck is what furniture and fixtures will be on the deck and where? A table or two perhaps? And how many chairs? Will there be any loungers, BBQ, swings, hammock, benches, planters, spa, bars, kitchens, fireplaces, fire pits, gazebos, trellises, pergolas, serving trays, tables, or ponds? All of these items take up space and need to be placed in the design for proper sizing. The most common error in deck building and designing is making the deck too small. A deck too big will cost more than needed, but one too small just won't do the job! Knowing what you will use your deck for helps when planning it. A shaded private area to read will be quite different than the party area with the spa. Access into the yard is a major design decision and traffic flow needs to be considered. If you have had a deck before, consider what you liked and disliked about it, and apply those ideas to your new project.

The third major area that continues to lead to your final design is the dreaded budget. Pricing is a concern to think about early in your design planning, as this will set parameters on the extent of your project. The larger the deck, the more it will cost in time and material to construct. I tell my customers to build it the right size with money left over to add special features and touches. Using some of the great products out there now can lead to a deck that will last for over twenty years of problem-free service. We strongly suggest composite decking for the flooring. Who has time to sand and stain a deck every year or two? We also suggest stainless steel hardware for a deck that you want to last. Outdoor lighting built into a deck project makes a cozy evening environment and also keeps people from tripping on steps and level changes. The budget on a custom deck will probably cost 25-50% more than you hoped, but remember, it is much cheaper to do it right the first time than to build two or three decks over your lifetime in your home. When you consider maintenance costs and replacement costs every 10-15 years, it pays handsomely to do it right the first time.

The last area to consider in our design process is your personal preference. No two people are alike, so no two decks should be either. The idea of this book is to open your imagination to the endless possibilities for your own deck project. Borrow an idea here and another idea there, and soon you will have something truly unique.

Have fun designing your dream deck and good luck.

Tom Jacques
President, Hickory Dickory Decks
Head Office:
115 Dundas Street West
Highway #5, Clappisons Corners
Flamborough, Ontario L9H 7L6
(905) 689-4774; (800) 263-4774
(905) 689-9753 FAX
www.decks.ca
www.hickorydickorydecks.com

Chapter 1
All Shapes & Sizes

This grandiose outdoor environment is made of maintenance free Xccent™ Decking. Stretching from one end of the house to the other, the deck provides a variety of areas from which to enjoy the fresh air and open views.

Graceful curves add interest to this deck's design, while privacy screens provide protection from public views. Multiple levels establish different deck zones for eating, cooking, sunbathing, and lounging. Cedar railings and trim contrast with gray maintenance free decking, but with age will also turn gray.

This shapely deck sits close to the ground without any railings. A trellis above the grilling station will keep the hot sun from scorching the cook on hot summer afternoons.

Gray maintenance free decking complements the gray brick of this home, while plants along the deck's edges add life and a greater connection to nature.

The design of this small, simple deck gains refinement with a circular edge that spills out onto the lawn.

This deck's circular design gives it the air of a grand balcony. This decking material is Procell, and it has a lifetime warranty to never splinter or crack.

Dark trim defines the curves of this low-lying deck. Circular steps extend at an angle and maintain the deck's shapely look. This is an example of low maintenance Trex® decking.

A wide, circular step outlines the edge of this deck with planks set at a perpendicular angle. Planters overflowing with gorgeous summer flowers create a welcoming entry onto the deck from the lawn.

An attractive poolside deck follows the curve of a pool's cement skirting.

Here, the deck's octagonal extension is like an island surrounded by a sea of landscaping. This is the original cedar deck outside our head office. It has just been replaced with maintenance free decking after sixteen years.

This deck features two octagonal areas. The first is raised to meet the door, while the second area sits below the rest of the deck to create a cozy eating nook.

Boards of maintenance free decking laid in an octagonal pattern are surrounded by steps along the deck's outer edges.

This three level Trex® deck is the third project we completed for this customer.

Whether inset or raised, an octagonal shape in a deck's layout designates a separate zone while adding interest.
This is the first VEKAdeck™ built in Canada.

Rather than ending in boring, square steps, this deck was designed with steps that splay out into the yard.

You won't find any squares on this deck. Different geometric shapes and angles make for an exciting layout.

An umbrella set in the middle of this octagonal deck extension provides the perfect gathering place around which friends can meet and escape the sun's midday heat.

A rectangular house gets dressed up with the help of a geometrically designed deck.

A variety of levels and angled edges create room-like spaces on this outdoor deck environment, made with clear British Columbia cedar.

The table can be moved to this deck's octagonal area during larger parties.

Octagons at the corners and center of this deck make a pattern like ripples on water for a graceful and welcoming design.

This deck is long and narrow along the edge of the house then blossoms into an octagon at the end to provide a roomier space for a table and chairs.

For homeowners that don't entertain large groups of friends, this octagonal deck provides the perfect location to enjoy the great outdoors, lawn style.

Boards placed diagonally add interest and warn of a change in this deck's level.

Built around the trunk of a tree, this irregularly shaped deck provides seating located in shaded and sunny areas.

The angles of this deck complement the geometric character of the home that it adorns.

An angled landing makes up for the difference in height between the sliding doors of the kitchen and enclosed porch.

Darker boards adorn the edge of this angled deck to add contrast and decoration.

Steps in a V-shape are accessible from the two major areas of this deck and are accented by a planter where they meet.

Landscaping along the edge of this house defined this deck's shape, which runs parallel to the house before extending out into the lawn.

Railings and a privacy screen act as walls to create a room-like space on this deck, which also features a section that openly unfolds into the yard.

An expansive deck acts as two with its unique shape and construction. Rather than create a deck that was too large, this design features two separate deck areas connected by a narrow walkway to create a more welcoming outdoor space.

The curves of this deck replace straight lines and sharp corners, and contrast elegantly against the angles of the home.

The shape formed by the walls of this house called for a distinctive deck design. The call
was answered with the inclusion of a pergola and arbor, as well as by a custom layout
design.

Chapter 2
Beauty in the Details

Balustrades

Turned balusters in the deck railing bestow an interior quality to this outdoor room.

Balusters in a distinctive shape add luxury to this deck. The contrast of white against a natural wood floor provides an elegant look that complements the traditional style of a brick home.

Low to the ground, this deck's extension was built without railings, providing open, unobstructed access to the surrounding yard. Meanwhile, closer to the house, balustrades replace walls to create the feeling of a protective room.

Decorative post caps contrast with maintenance free decking and impart a refined style to this outdoor space.

Curved balusters add dimension and flourish to this deck's railing.

Tempered Glass Rail

Tempered glass and black railings give this deck a sleek, architectural aesthetic.

More traditional cedar railings surround tempered glass to form a dynamic, contemporary look. The decking is gray colored Dexx.™

This kind of railing provides open, unobstructed views from a second story deck while echoing the home's architectural style.

Tempered glass rails complement gray maintenance free Dexx™, providing dramatic contrast to light-colored pine railings and privacy walls.

Bungalow-style shingles attractively adorn the walls embracing a smaller-sized deck. Taking the place
of railings, the walls add an architectural element that makes this outdoor space feel like a living room.

Metal

Dark metal balusters and post caps topped in black make an attractive pairing with black and tan outdoor furniture.

A bench marks the angled edges of a maintenance free deck along with a metal and wood balustrade .

This WeatherBest® deck provides lots of room for large get-togethers.

Metal balusters have a less bulky appearance than their wooden counterparts, offering sleek minimalism to contemporary deck design.

No Balustrades

A deck with geometric interest and a low stature features benches instead of balustrades.
The Procell decking is inlaid with Brazilian hardwood, which makes for a beautiful deck.

Because this deck sits low to the ground, local standards allow the absence of balustrades. Steps spread out from the
deck's lower level as they descend to the ground, while the upper level boasts a planter and benches to mark its edges.

The Underworld of Decks

Boarded Walls

A narrow deck was built to make up for the difference in height between the ground and the home's sliding glass doors. Boards placed to hide the area underneath the deck from view provide a neat appearance.

Maintenance free decking in a dark color wraps around the foot of this deck and contrasts with lighter deck flooring. A black metal railing creates a refined look.

A solid white wall beneath the balustrade gives the impression of sturdiness. A door hinged there hides a handy storage area.

Cedar boards rise to meet the floor of a deck's octagonal extension.

Lattice Screens

Thin latticework makes for a more delicate screen between the yard and the deck's underside.
The look is a good match for an impressive brick home.

White lattice complements the deck's white maintenance free floor
made of E-Z Deck®.

This type of lattice runs vertically and horizontally, an attractive alternative to more typical diagonally oriented lattice.

The Bare Beams

Milled logs attractively support the weight of a second story deck, meeting a wooden base at the ground that outlines a basement's walk out patio.

Circular support beams give this deck a rustic appearance when viewed from ground level.
Concrete pavers form a sturdy walkway and landing beneath the deck.

Supports dressed in aluminum columns establish a finished, formal look. The decking is maintenance free Nexwood®.

Gray maintenance free decking and white support columns pair elegantly with a patio fashioned from concrete pavers.

This cedar deck's six-by-six support columns offer a more utilitarian – and less costly – approach to deck design.

Here, six-by-six support columns get extra help and ornamentation from load-bearing brackets.

Steppin' Out

These steps give a grand impression from the backyard.

This white decking is fiberglass composite E-Z Deck®.

Steps in the shape of three octagonal sides look great day or night.

Lights on deck steps are primarily safety features, but
add nighttime allure and drama to any deck's design.

A ramp was built to accommodate this home's wheelchair-bound resident.

A traditional set of wide stairs adorned with planters leads from deck to walkway.

These angled steps provide access to both sides of a diverging path.

A low-level deck was fashioned with two customary steps to meet the grass below.

Wide, angled steps give shape to a lengthy deck, and can be approached from different areas of the yard.

Angled steps seem to float out from the edge of this gray maintenance free deck.

In a yard cramped for space, steps leading from a second story deck to the ground below angle back towards the house.

Here, a sprawling lawn allows for steps that stretch to the grass in a straight line and end in a landing.

These steps lead deck dwellers straight to the backyard and lake. The deck is made from maintenance free Nexwood® and the railing is cedar.

Spiraling staircases curve towards the ground with style and grace, an exciting element of modern deck design. Not only do they look good – spiral staircases are extreme space-savers too.

Chapter 3
Multi-Level Decks

Steps curve from one level to another on a deck with architectural presence and generous amounts of space.

This deck seems to unfold naturally from the home into the yard. Cedar boards along the wall on the lower level transition from the brick of the home's walls to the deck floor.

A cute cottage in the woods provides a sprawling deck where homeowners can commune with nature from the comfort of an architectural space.

Puddle-like steps spill onto the lawn, as metal balustrades descend like the walls of a temple towards the home.

Lights create accents along the length of narrow steps and sprawling levels of deck. Flowers the color of autumn leaves create further interest. This entire deck is made with low maintenance Xtendex®.

Summer blossoms hang lush, like decorative cornices that distinguish between the halls and entrances of grand palaces; like earrings and necklaces that hang from fine ladies.

Lights can help develop a sense of place, illuminating walls into the dark of night.

The glow of strategically placed lights among layers of deck infuse the dark of night with romance, mystery, and a sense of comfort.

Window placement and size can serve as the basis for an attractive and practical deck layout.

The angles of a deck's shape unfold dramatically to create architectural interest.

The home's architecture, deck's features, and even the outdoor furniture coordinate, a divine combination.
Tall bushes guard the deck's lower level, which opens directly onto the lawn surrounding it.

Black metal railings and posts act as unobtrusive barriers between different levels of deck with the help of tempered glass. In addition to amplifying the perceived amount of space on the upper level, this modern version of the balustrade complements the architectural style of the home's windows.

Placing the grill on a higher level than the outdoor dining area helps to avoid the discomfort of barbecue smoke in guests' faces.

Rounded steps create separate levels of deck, with plants offering a natural distinction of space.

Intersecting angles and levels create dramatically shaped areas of deck. Privacy screens offer shelter to a group of seats below the pergola.

The back of this deck looks out into dense woods, which offers shelter in the place of a privacy screen or other outdoor wall.
Flower filled planters border steps – rising like the hanging gardens of Babylon.

Plants obscure outdoor views from frequently used rooms, offering a natural sanctuary and the feeling of intimacy.

A home's orientation towards the sun is an important consideration when planning a deck. Here, shadows of a westerly-facing home fall on the deck during the afternoon, offering relief from the hot sun just in time to invite friends over for a cookout.

Deck levels are sometimes established only with single steps.

The rounded corners of this deck display an art deco sensibility. The decking is WeatherBest®.

A back door's landing falls in layers past a hot tub on the way to its final destination, a cement-skirted pool.

Edges of this expansive deck cascade into the lawn's stone border. The entire project is made with Monarch™ decking.

The grill was placed on the landing outside the kitchen door to facilitate easy access from the cook's command center.

Just one step creates the feeling of a completely different room on this modest yet becoming deck.

A wall at the foot of the stairs plays host to a bench and two planters, providing a welcoming, cozy space.

Maintenance free Life Long® Decking boards lay in parallel directions on each level of this deck. A full bouquet of leaves offers shelter to hot tub users, who get to bathe among treetops.

The boards of this deck's lower level create energy with their diagonal orientation.

Chapter 4
Extras

A quaint garden door, curved bottom trellis, and flowering plants afford an idyllic atmosphere to this outdoor sanctuary. Multiple levels of deck hide the base of the hot tub, which seems to float above the ground.

A bar can be placed to jut out of a wall, or along the edge of the deck. Here, the high perch allows a view of the action in the pool.

A wall was constructed as backup for this second-story bar. Accent lights placed on the wall help keep friends' drinks straight on those long summer evenings, and plexiglas panels convey the sensation of sitting in treetops.

This deck is an outdoor pleasure quarter, complete with bar, hot tub, and a gorgeous design. Trellises line the deck's edge to create the impression of a room with no ceiling. The hot tub's pyramid-like roof creates atmosphere in unison with architectural details like decorative brackets and a sun patterned baluster.

Special evenings happen at the edge of a firepit constructed right into the deck, which features all the amenities of home, only outdoors. We completed this very large project in our earlier years.

Benches mark the edges of this dockside deck, complete with matching picnic table.

Hittin' the Bench

A bench along the landscaped edge of this deck invites passersby to sit and enjoy the company of trees, birds, and sky.

A bench guards each side of this deck's edge, with delightful landscaping below to add interest to the lawn.

The Power of Planters

Planters planted at the foot of the deck's entrance greet yard-goers with a cheerful burst of summer blossoms.

On a small deck, a built-in planter can save a lot of space while offering natural décor.

Planters & Benches

This configuration of a planter-flanked bench adds décor and one more seat to the deck.

Planters help make the visual transition from steps to bench an attractive one. A privacy screen meets the bench's other side.

Three symmetrically placed planters break up the continuity of benches, providing interest.

Each spring, flowers and greenery add life to the deck, creating a lively entrance from the yard.

Planters punctuate an extensive deck.

Sun Block

Perched on the lower-level circular extension of the deck, this shade-bearing structure protects diners from the sun during outdoor meals.

The addition of a roof turns a deck into a porch.

A gabled roof provides shade during the day, reflecting the light from a hanging fixture at night.

A roof gives the home's rear entrance a more striking appearance.

This back porch is beautiful enough to appear on the home's more public façade. No detail was spared in its design, which makes for a charming addition to the home.

Awnings provide shade, but on cooler days can be retracted to let warm sun through.

Trellises

A trellis features grid-patterned lattice-work as its base, which provides a sense of safety and architecture to this home's outdoor environment.

Plants hang from crisscrossing segments of trellis like green and flowered jewels and chains.

The shade of a trellis and lattice wall makes an ideal partner for benches.

Here, no lattice wall was included in the design of a trellis. Instead, the deck's bench gets an upgrade with its lattice back.

Curtains made from weatherproof textile hang from a trellis in an outdoor living room, creating the impression of a sliding glass door.

Hanging plants are easier to manage than climbing plants, and make an attractive addition to any deck.

Pergolas

This pergola emphasizes the home's shape and distinguishes between different "rooms" on the deck.

The crisscrossing roof of a pergola provides architecture and shade to outdoor meals. In order to save space, flower-filled window boxes were chosen rather than planters. Plants hanging in baskets would also add décor without occupying valuable space.

Structural elements balance within a harmonious design that combines the natural and built environment.

The view from under a pergola is shaded from sun, the perfect place to sip a mid-afternoon drink.
Although a patio sits below, cedar was used as a border to hide the pool's side that sits above ground.

A small deck and pergola define the transition between home and lawn.

Grape vines climb the columns that support a pergola. They will grow into a canopy, offering shade – and grapes – to those beneath.

Design-savvy lights glorify deck "walls" with strategically placed fixtures. They also illuminate this pergola ceiling, providing security and privacy to those underneath.

Decorative, load-bearing brackets and jigsawed beams add style and interest to a deck with all the amenities of home – even separate dining, lounging, and cooking areas. The door of a nearby gate echoes the pattern created by crossbeams, a privacy screen mirrored below the pergola on the deck's opposite side.

On this deck, the area below the pergola houses a hot tub and a swinging bench – the perfect place to spend an autumn evening.

Pergolas provide shade not only to the area of deck below, but to the house it borders as well.

A bench wraps around the edge of the deck that falls in close proximity to a pergola, forming a fresh-air sanctuary.

The privacy screen of a pergola-covered deck also provides shade during summer's late evenings.

Privacy Screens

Straight, board walls form a screen that crests in a central Palladian arch.

This privacy screen is slatted to let the air and light through.

The screens on this deck decorate and protect from neighbors' glances, offering a sense of security with their architectural qualities.

The screens on this deck offer one hundred percent privacy, and a cool, contemporary look.

Diagonally placed boards with lattice-work atop form a geometric pattern.

Latticework placed like a grid is used as a wall, providing the utmost privacy and air circulation to a road-facing deck.

An arched panel in this deck's wall mirrors the shape of similar arches in the home's windows and doors. The lattice-work panel contrasts with adjacent walls of diagonally-placed boards.

This deck's privacy screen was built from slatted and latticework panels.

An upward-spiraling planter is the only detail adorning this deck's privacy screen that wasn't built with the rest of the deck.

Privacy screens can run the length of a straight wall...

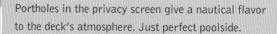

Portholes in the privacy screen give a nautical flavor to the deck's atmosphere. Just perfect poolside.

This screen hugs the corner and hides the hot tub.

Privacy screens can occupy large expanses, or smaller sections of deck to cut down on cost.

This privacy screen hides steps that climb down behind it.

These beautiful wooden screens don't just belong at the edge of deck. They can also be built to border a stone patio.

The wood of this screen bends to follow the patio's curve.

Chapter 5
Waterside Designs

Pool Skirting Decks

A house on a hill features an above ground pool. Thanks to brilliant deck design, though, this backyard's watery wonder looks like it sits underground.

An elevated deck hides the above ground portion of this pool, too.

This home's deck stretches from the house all the way to the pool, with different levels indicating areas with separate functions.

A wooden deck surrounds this watery oasis, which feels like a natural grotto with its lush landscaping.

Steps leading from the kitchen door to the deck mimic the shape of an octagon motif that lends interest.

Tall walls built with the deck offer protection and a sense of security, creating an outdoor pool room.

Maintenance free E-Z Deck® decking and beautiful cedar were both used to complete this outdoor project – which features a gazebo as well as pool-skirting and second-story decks.

A small deck was built to meet the edge of a partially above ground pool, which was surrounded by wood and planters for a more attractive appearance. Lights on the stairs and privacy wall illuminate for safety and appeal when it's dark. Notice the gorgeous privacy wall design.

Decks Near Pools

This deck's shape follows the curve of a pool, rolling like a wave of water.

Landscaping adorns the border between the deck and cement pool-skirting patio, providing a transition between the two areas. Notice the built-in planters that flank the deck's steps.

A narrow slab of deck connects the dining area with the cook's outdoor command center. Running the length of the house, the deck maintains a sense of continuity and harmony next to the concrete patio that borders the pool.

Tall trees shelter this outdoor environment from the neighbors' views. With all its amenities, this deck is reminiscent of resort living.

This home's deck is basically an extension of the gazebo, which houses an outdoor eating area. A beautiful concrete paver patio was fashioned for lounging.

In this backyard, the pool was constructed at quite a distance from the house. The deck extends in dramatic angles all the way to the pool's concrete skirt to make it feel more like part of the home. The TREX® decking never needs staining, so its owners can sit back and enjoy a maintenance free summer.

A small deck hugs the house and empties onto the pool's patio. The deck provides seating and a higher perspective.

A maintenance free deck provides a place for the adults to sit and relax while kids splash around in the pool.

An elevated deck provides an almost-aerial view of the pool below, and interest to the backyard's built landscape.

The lawn makes for a texturally interesting area between deck and pool skirt, and feels good on bare feet.

Hot Tubs

Outdoor dinner guests favor the hot tub as their after-dinner treat.

A taller level of deck surrounded by railings is kept separate from the hot tub, which sits on the ground and is sheltered from view by a privacy screen.

A small, elevated deck was constructed to facilitate easy hot tub entry, and make up for the difference in height between the ground and the home's back entrance.

Some digging was required to get this hot tub to sit flush with the deck.

This hot tub was incorporated into the deck's design rather than placing it, like an afterthought, at the deck's perimeter.

Soakers step up before stepping inside the hot tub. Its sides are covered in WeatherBest® Decking to keep a consistent look with the maintenance free deck.

The taller area surrounding this hot tub provides the perfect place to keep drinks during long soaks.

In order to keep hot tub use discreet and intimate, privacy screens and walls were included in these decks' designs.

A privacy screen and pergola provide a much-desired sense of shelter and security when soaking in the hot tub.

In this backyard, the hot tub was placed far way from the house, necessitating the construction of this outdoor room.
The distance from the house offers sanctuary and seclusion to hot tub goers.

Hot tub privacy is not a concern with the addition of these sight-impairing screens. They also add a contemporary flair to this deck's design.

Steps made from Xtendex® decking ascend to a hot-tub surround, guarded from view by a cedar privacy lattice.

Lights add drama to this favorite nighttime hotspot.

Accent lights add décor to this hot tub area at night, creating a sense of space and comfort.

A Palladian arch tops this privacy screen, adding architectural detail to this outdoor environment.
WeatherBest® Decking never needs staining and has great traction when wet—an ideal feature
around spas.

Chapter 6
Landscaping

Around the Deck

This TREX® deck makes a grander impression with the addition of lush landscaping around its perimeter. A stone patio creates a walkway that connects the separate hot tub area to the deck and home. Crossing over a basement entry, a bridge adds whimsy to the outdoor ensemble.

Bumped up against a hill, this deck features boulders along its edge for an earthy, primitive feel.

A stone patio and abundant plantings make for an attractive transition between deck and lawn.

Rocks set the stage for a small, manmade pond bordered by a variety of flowering and leafy plants. Two slabs of stone cross over the shallow construction, where time can be spent watching water ripple in even the softest breeze.

Water features enhance any deck's design and enrich the outdoor experience with the relaxing murmur of a gentle cascade.

A narrow strip of bright summer flowers were planted along the edge of this small deck, which also features a shade-giving tree.

Here, a path of concrete pavers snakes around to the deck from the driveway, bordered on both sides by landscaping.

Landscaped areas add décor to a deck, providing natural adornments to an outdoor built environment.

Two saplings mark the entrance of the deck from the backyard, which ends at the intersection of landscaping, arching paths, and lawn. This entire deck is made with white maintenance free vinyl.

Trees bordering a deck's lawn-facing side will grow to provide shade and privacy.
A short wall attractively marks the edge of the landscaped area.

Deck steps splay out into a gray stone border. Only a small area off the blocked edge of deck features a burst of landscaping.

A pocket of flowers planted in between adjacent deck and patio creates a multicolored pillow of blossoms.

Two levels of deck intersect at an angle to preserve this tree. Decks can also be built right around the circumference of a tree, incorporating it into the overall design.

A variety of plants were spread out in two landscaped areas at the edge of this deck.

Flowers spread out in a carpet at the edge of a deck-bordering patio.

Here, a deck's extension floats like an island in a landscaped sea. The Procell decking ensures that these homeowners will enjoy many maintenance free seasons.

The harvest season brings an end to lush summer foliage, but these evergreen bushes soften the look of the deck's edge all year 'round.

On the Deck

At the height of summer, baskets and planters overflow with flowers planted in early spring.

Flowers punctuate a deck in color. Soakers have to be careful not to splash into the planters that border the hot tub.

Here, plants mark the deck's edge like pony walls constructed of leaves and blossoms.

Flowers in built-in planters, clay pots, and hanging baskets enliven and add charm to this deck.

A large pot was placed at the angled intersection of a set of steps, marking the space like a column.

Potted plants on the deck create a welcoming outdoor space.

Chapter 7
Outdoor Structures

Gazebos offer shaded sanctuary on sun soaked decks.

Boards were cut and placed to form an octagon-shaped pattern on the gazebo's floor. The gazebo's
placement next to the hot tub contributes a feeling of safety to soakers.

A patio's gazebo looks like a pagoda. The design would be attractive on a deck as well.

Decorative brackets and railings were chosen for a gazebo that features built-in furniture.

The gazebo looks out over the deck's firepit, as well as a small coi pond filled with lily pads.

Gazebos can be open to the elements, or feature protective screens and doors.

This poolside gazebo offers shade and protection from pesky insects.

Decorative details in the gazebo's design add whimsy to this backyard environment. A small shed lends balance and a convenient storage space. This entire project was constructed using maintenance free Xtendex®.

Secluded at the edge of woods, and the backyard, this pagoda-shaped gazebo offers sanctuary and a place to commune with the natural world.

A string of blue lights around the gazebo creates an exciting effect during evening get-togethers.

Even a gazebo set below the main deck and away from the house was furnished with electricity so a light fixture could be installed in the ceiling.

This lit gazebo provides a warm and comfortable gathering place after the sun goes down. During the day, the structure protects from the powerful sun.

A small cabana at the edge of the pool offers storage space and cover from bright summer sunshine.

At the edge of a patio, this structure really feels like an interior space.

A white gazebo matches white maintenance free decking. A door repeats the decorative pattern of the structure's bracket.

Perched above a dramatically landscaped backyard, this gazebo enjoys half solid, half screened-in walls.
This deck was the first install of WeatherBest® Decking in Canada.

This outdoor deck structure provides lots of privacy, while maintaining the fresh-air feeling of the outdoors.

A bar was attached to the exterior of this storage structure — the perfect feature for outdoor-loving entertainers.

This bar has a more sturdy, permanent look with solid walls underneath the bar top. I'll take a cold one, please.

The deck was fashioned with a mini shed for storage of pool equipment.

Though not a part of any deck in these images, arbors and gates are other structures that can be built to enhance the look of outdoor areas.